The Tattoo Training Guide
How to Create a Six Figure Income
A complete guide for Beginner & Advanced Artists

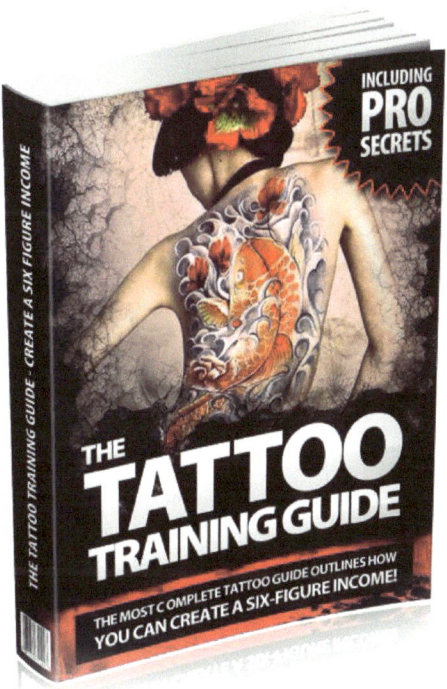

THE ULTIMATE TATTOO TRAINING GUIDE

How to Create a Six Figure Income!

Contents

Introduction

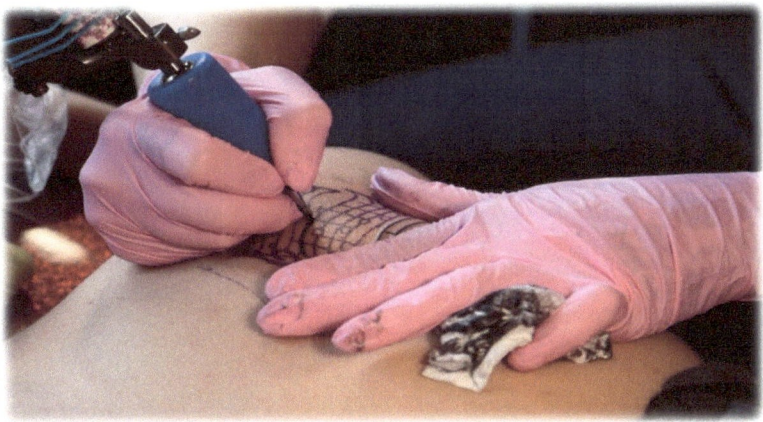

   The most important thing to take in to consideration when learning how to be a tattoo artist, is to make sure you are learning the proper & safest way. The importance of the proper precautions affects the outcome of your work in more ways than you probably imagine. Not only do proper techniques when actually tattooing play a huge role, but also preparation, quality of tools, skill, cleanliness, all play a huge role in the final outcome of your work. This book is designed to show you the proper techniques and precautions to get you started in tattooing. Please note: This book is not to turn you in to a professional tattoo artist after reading. Its purpose is to give you a basic introduction and overview on tattooing. This book is everything you need to know before you get started, though it is recommended that you head to your local tattoo shop and ask questions, learn from their business and see how day to day things go in an actual tattoo shop. A lot of people think tattooing is an easy profession to just pick up and do. Although there are a lot of artistically talented people out there who can pick up a pen or pencil and draw a masterpiece, tattooing is not only an art form but it also takes a lot technique and practice! A lot of people give up and quit before they are actually able to grasp the proper tools & technique and knowledge to grow at their craft.

Tattoo takes talent, patience & a love for the art. Acquiring the proper tools is very necessary to get good results out of your work, tattooing is not something you want to do on a penny pinching budget. Getting the best quality products will definitely help your chances of getting a beautiful piece of art in the end.

Developing a good initial reputation is a good start to a great business. Be sure to start off on the right foot & be professional in every way possible, you will be rewarded with returning customers and a growing clientele. For people who are getting their first tattoo, it's important to give them a positive, exciting & comfortable vibe, so they not only fall in love with that art of tattoos but will want to come back to your shop and get more work done by you!

Customers always want to know that they are getting highest grade work possible, a tattoo is something that lasts for a lifetime, so not only do you want it to look good, but you want their memory to be a great one and something that will make them happy when they look back at it 20 years from getting it.

We will be going over a lot of methods here and by the time you're done reading this you should be able to apply these methods and without a doubt start making yourself 6 figures in a year or more.

Chapter 1: Knowing your tools & Equipment

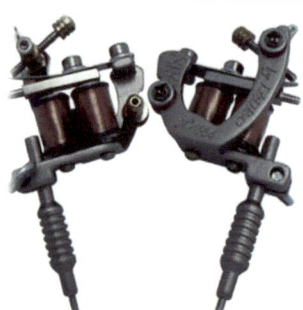

Before you begin tattooing, you will need to learn and understand all of your tools. There is a general guideline when it comes to the tattooing essentials; most artists list will be the same with the exception of a few who will probably have a few specific tools of their preference.

Here is a list of the most common essentials you will need to get you started:

Multiple Tattoo Machines:
Most Tattoo artists use multiple Tattoo machines, using different machines for different tasks. You usually learn what works best for you as you go along with different projects, using different machines for Lines, shading & coloring.

Foot Switch: This is used to control your machine; it allows you to control it with your foot, leaving your hand free to control the machines direction.

Various Tattoo Parts: This is usually different Tattoo machine parts, one common parts is a rubber band.

Feeler Gauge: A feeler gauge is used for making adjustments for contact points.
Power Supply: This is your main power source to run your machines.

Summary: It's best to not go cheap when buying your tattoo equipment. It will save you a lot of time and anguish later. The worst thing ever is to have your tattoo machine and/or power supplies go out in the middle of a tattoo. This is not only embarrassing but it is extremely unprofessional and you client may decide that next time they want to go to someone who has invested in their machines! Spend the extra money to buy good quality tattoo machines and power supplies.

Needle Accessories

Regular Needle Bars: Used to hold the main needle group.

Needle Jig and Needle bar Jig: Used to make the right needle group and keep the placement of the groups with the bars. When starting out your teacher may require you to make your very own needles using a jig, yes it's kind of outdated in 2012-2013, but many shops require it to help develop your knowledge & understanding of your machine and how it works.
Soldering Gun and Stainless Solder: Used to fuse or solder the needles together and to connect the needles to the bars.

Shop Furniture & equipment

Work Table: Most states require a Stainless Steel work table, for sanitation & cleanliness reasons. This is where you will hold most of your supplies during the process of your clients tattoo session.

Personal Chair: It's important for the artist to also be comfortable; having your own personal chair that is adjusted to your personal preference is the best way. Usually people prefer with wheels, but whatever works for you or your situation is what's best.

Customer Chair: Clients are sometimes sitting for several hours straight while they are getting tattooed; investing in a nice comfortable & sturdy chair is worth the investment and will help keep your client comfortable & relaxed.

Flat padded Bench (Massage Table): You want to make sure to use a padded bench because customers getting back or leg tattoos will be laying there for long periods of time, in an already uncomfortable position. Always make sure you wrap this chair in plastic as you are doing the tattoo, to be 100% sure that no body fluids from your client get on the table.

Light: Usually a nice flexible fluorescent light works great, it provides a great source of light, clarity, and it doesn't really get hot, so you can move it as close as needed. You definitely need a good light to be able to see what you're doing!

Paper Towels & Trash Can: There are two main brands when it comes to tattooing, Bounty & Viva. Both work great, but lately I personally have been using Viva, Not only are they very adsorbent but there very soft on the skin. Therefore they have become a favorite with some artists.

Sterilization Equipment

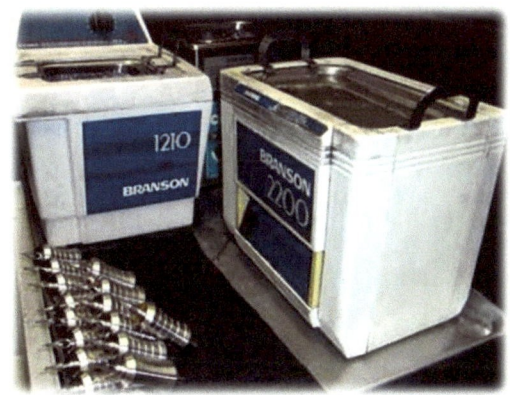

Autoclave (Stericlave): This is an absolute essential part of your equipment. This is a device that provides heat, steam & pressure which will disinfect & sterilize your equipment. Also make sure you check with the health department, sometimes they will want the autoclave to be special certified or they ask for a particular model, it may even have to be inspected by local authorities.

Autoclave bags: This is where you store your freshly sterilized needles in the bag, being sure that they are not contaminated with anything. It's always good practice to pull them straight out of the bag in front of the customer, assuring them that it has been sterilized. This again, allows them to be feel comforted knowing they are getting a freshly sterilized tool.

Ultrasonic Tray and Machine Holder: This is a tray that can be submersed in the Ultrasonic Cleaner with the tools attached. These will break up all the caked up ink on your equipment after its done being used, preparing it to be thoroughly washed and autoclaved

Tattoo Machine Rack: Simple rack to hold unused tattoo machines. This is good to have handy during the tattoo session, so you don't have to leave your station to get other machines for different sections.

Germicidal Solution: A simple solution that doesn't rust or doesn't sterilize, but keeps equipment clean.

A very commonly used germicidal is Madicide, in the last few years.

There are many different brands and types of germicidal solutions available.

Medical Equipment

Needle Trays: Stainless steel trays used to place needles.

Always be sure to use stainless steel, it's great for sanitation, it looks great and it's very easy to clean.

Various Spray Bottles: Most people will say to have two bottles, one for a 1/3 soap to water ratio and the other bottle will hold isopropyl alcohol. A lot of people are turning to Nitrile bottles, being that they are inexpensive and easy to autoclave.

Small Glass Jars: It's always good to have several small jars available, You will need a lot of these for all your different small supplies, perishables such as ink cups, cotton swabs, etc.

Various Antibiotic Ointments and Solutions: Used for wiping client after tattoo is complete. Most common is A+D Ointment, sometimes Neosporin.

*BE SURE TO PURCHASE THE GEL NOT THE CREAM.

Though Neosporin is great for cuts & scrapes, it's not good for tattoo healing process.

Green Soap: This is used for cleanup and preparation. Please note that this soap is NOT used for sterilization purposes. It only helps in the tattoo procedure to clean the skin.

Disposable razors: Always shave area where you will be working, this will prevent ingrown hairs as well as clean the area of interruptions while tattooing. Use quality razors. "BIC" Razors usually the most common and they are very inexpensive.

8

Various wraps, bandages & medical tapes: This is used for the initial wrapping of the customers tattoo after you are done. Saran wrap is best, it gets the job done and it's very inexpensive.

Rubbing Alcohol and Pads: Usually used to wipe down client before placing stencil on skin. This helps keep the work area clean to prevent any smudges in ink from the stencil and/or tattoo machine.

Tongue Depressors: Used for the application of various ointments.

Sharp Scissors: Stainless steel SHARP hospital scissors.
It's always good to make sure these are stainless steel, it makes them a lot easier for sanitation reasons, it also makes it easier to sharpen them.

Latex Gloves: Never begin the tattoo process without latex or some type of surgical glove. Period. Body fluids getting on your hands are completely unsafe. Also make sure you have some nitrile gloves on hand these days we have people that are allergic to latex, so you want to make sure you accommodate those clients as well

Art and Stencil Supplies

Various Colored Inks: A variety of ink, colors, usually a lot of black as this is the most common color in outlining & shading.

Ink Cups: Recommend using disposables to prevent cross contamination.
These days, it's almost mandatory to use disposable cups; there are too many germs out there to dispose clients of un-sanitary ink.

Ink Bottles: These are four ounce sized with a twist top. Always be sure to have a lot of ink handy, it's also always a good idea to use high quality ink, low quality ink leaves for a ugly looking tattoo!

Cup Holder: Used to keep all ink caps in place.
This allows you to be organized, and prevents any ink spills on your clothes or anywhere else.

The Ultimate Tattoo Training Guide

Flash: These are various sheets of flash tattoo designs.

Watercolors and Pencils: Used to color flash sheets.

Chapter 2: Knowing your Tattoo Machines

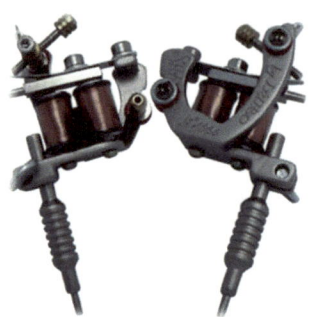

Knowing and understanding the way your tattoo machine works, is as important as a marine soldier knowing the ins and outs of his rifle. Knowing how your machine works will allow you to understand it and understand how to work it and make sure that it is set up correctly and hopefully be able to prevent any malfunctions in the process of doing your tattoo. Most machines all include the same things: These include standard contact points, the location where the needle goes through, power supply as well as other parts such as front and rear springs, contact caps, soldering lug, binding post, machine frame, needle tube, band hook and needle bar.

A tattoo machine is pretty much a machine that has a very fast moving needle that moves up and down in a very fast paced motion, usually too fast for your eye to even be able to catch it moving, it looks like it's sitting still. The needle penetrates the skin just enough to allow the ink to get under the top layer of skin, while the artist controls it like an artist would control a pencil. Having a properly set up high quality is very important, it'll leave the tattoo looking clean, consistent and leave clean lines and good shading.

Using Your Tattoo Machine

Now that you have an understanding of the machine and how it works, you can begin tattooing, but because the machine only helps the artist make beautiful tattoos, it is the job of the individual to know how to hold the machine properly and maneuver the machine in different positions upon tattooing different body parts, areas & positions.

One of the first things to keep in mind is the size and the weight of the machine, this makes a huge difference when it comes to comfort so you want to be sure to have a comfortable machine. A lot of people prefer to use lighter machines to do lines and heavier machines to do shading, this allows you to be able to apply pressure and control the machine as needed. When it comes down to it, it really is all preference, whatever works best for you, the artist, is the best way to go about picking your machines.

When gripping the tattoo machine you need to actually grip it around the needle tube. To do this you will grab hold of the knurled grip much like you would hold a pencil. Be sure the open side of the needle tip is facing away from you. It may take a little time to develop the muscles to be able to control the machine comfortably. It's important that before taking on big projects, like a back piece or a chest piece, that you have the ability to be able to hold the machine for a long period of time without getting tired and without losing focus/control.

The palm of your hand should be resting on the surface of the skin; much like the way you would do if you were writing on the customer's skin with a pen. This allows your hand to have a solid foundation to control the machine with the rest of your fingers. The palm of your hand can be used to swivel and turn the tattoo machine on the skin. Actually, learning to pivot and turn effectively is going to make your designs a whole lot easier to master.

You will need to tilt the tattoo machine at a 45-degree angle, with the butt of the machine dropping towards the skin. When you have the grip on the tattoo machine, naturally your palm is going to rest on the skin. This is completely normal. As I mentioned earlier, you will use the palm and heel to pivot, move and control the tattoo machine. Learning how to properly angle the machine allows you to be able to make an even amount of ink throughout the tattoo and it allows the ink to be able to sit in the skin. If you point in a straight up and down direction, the ink often will bounce back at you, leaving only some ink inside the skin, and most of it all over the place, leaving a sloppy and blurry looking tattoo.

A few tips for holding your machine:

Proper angle: Holding the machine at a proper 45* angle is very important to making sure the ink gets under the skin properly.

Proper depth: Going too deep in the skin will cause a lot of pain and smearing of the ink. Not going deep enough will cause eventual fading ink.

Proper set up: I recommend learning taking apart and setting up your machine as much as possible until you can do it without really thinking about it. This will allow you to be productive when setting up and be able to do it in a comfortable and quick matter.

Palm placement: It's important to know how to use your palm for a guide, trying to free hand it with no support will cause instability and squiggly lines.
So practice using the side of your palm as a guide, or as a pivot point allowing you become solid at maneuvering.

Practice: Before trying to tattoo a person, you should have a lot of experience on artificial skins, a lot of drawing, and the strength and stamina to be able to control the machine for a long period of time. Using a family member or friend to apply the artificial skin on helps a lot, it allows you to get comfortable maneuvering and positioning yourself properly prior to doing a tattoo on a person's skin.

Chapter 3: Understanding How to Properly Use Needles

One of the most important parts of your machine is the needle, it is absolutely essential to have a fresh needle to have your final piece look its full potential. A used or dull needle will cause a lot

Tattoo needles are soldered onto needle bars. There are two types of needle bars. There are bars for lining and there are bars for shading. The Bar used for shading has a flat end where the needles are soldered and the lining bar is rounded on the end. Remember that lining bars are used to draw different thick outlines around objects or for creating borders for certain designs.

Needles also come in different sizes for the thickness of lines.
eg: one needles, three needles, four needles, five needles, etc.
Shading bars, of course, used for shading. The shading bars are designed to cover a large area with ink, while Lining bars vary in size, but are generally meant for drawing straight lines.

One of the scariest parts of beginning tattooing is learning how deep is deep enough and how deep is too deep. You want to be sure you are going deep enough to get a clean line but not too deep to cause pain, bleeding, and blurred lines and detail. Going to deep also often means it will scar and make it look faded after the tattoo heals, and should it ever need to be touched up, it will be painful to tattoo on scar tissue.

Tubes 12

You will also need a different tube for the different needle bars. They are constructed specifically to work with the type of needle bar and number of needles you intend to work with.
For example, if you're working with a 4-needle shading bar, then you'll need a 4-needle shading tube on your tattoo machine.
This applies to all other size bars as well. Matching them up correctly is very important.

There are also two sub groups within these groups of tubes (shaders or liners): round tip and square tip. Each tip has different qualities. For example, the round tip has very little problem with ink splatter but you might end up with a wider line when turning a sharp corner if not careful. The square tip is limited in the amount of movement but corners are usually sharp and defined. With a square tip; however, everything has to be in perfect alignment.

Disposable tube are really important these days, and for good reason the tubes made now are higher quality and are most of all disposable this cuts don't on sterilization issues, as you can finish the tattoo and just pitch these.

Chapter 4: Practice Skins

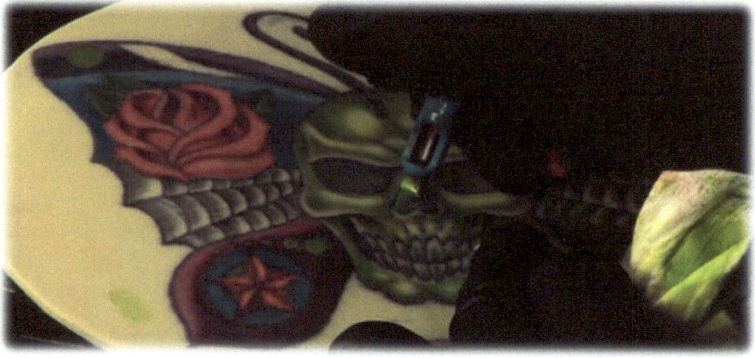

Tattooing on practice skins are a great way to practice. The skins are designed to provide the feel & texture as a person's body, you can buy them in different sizes and it's often a good idea to have a friend sit/lay down and position the skin on their body as if you were tattooing them. This is good hands on experience, helping you move in awkward positions, angles, and learning how to position your clients the best possible and comfortable way. This also allows you to be able to get in as many hours as you need before you are comfortable moving on to tattooing a friend or a client. Practice skins are very inexpensive, usually only a few dollars for a 6" x 8" piece, it's much better to mess one of these up then to mess up on a person's skin.

I would recommend starting out in an orderly fashion when it comes to perfecting your artistic skills. It's always good to get real good at doing outlines, as most of the time; this is the foundation of a tattoo. After you learn how to do solid, straight lines, you then want to get good at shading, this is a tough technique that takes a lot of experience and practice to perfect. Being a good at shading often is the difference an ok tattoo and a great tattoo, it brings out the character and the makes it stand out and look real.

Once you get good at shading, then comes adding in color. This takes a lot of knowledge & experience. A lot of colors clash when tattooing, meaning it takes a long time to get good at knowing what order to go in, what colors look good with what colors and if there is a particular order to go in when adding color. You always want to keep in mind also that peoples skin play a huge role in coloring and sometimes a customer may want a lot of color but their skin may not be the proper tone to compliment that color.

It's always good to know what colors work best on what skin tones, and if it seems as if it isn't going to work well, it will be best to let your customer in the most polite possible way, offering alternatives and other solutions so they don't think that you are just trying to get the easy way out.

Chapter 5: Learning about Tattoo Inks

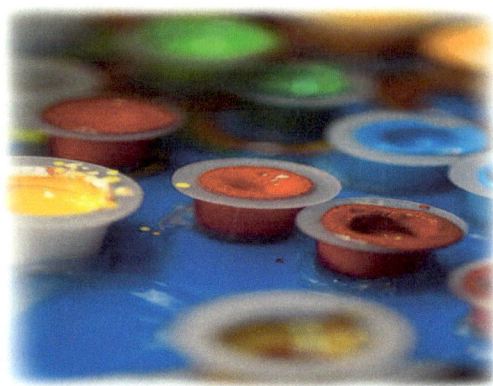

Choosing a good ink is extremely important in a tattoo. You could have a great design, machine set up, sketch and using a low quality, or poorly prepared ink will ruin the entire tattoo, leaving inconsistency, color smearing, and fading, which will leave a beautiful tattoo looking horrible. The difference in a decent tattoo and great tattoo could simply be the ink that you are using.

It's important to be knowledgeable of the different inks and what they are made of. Some may vary, but for the most parts, most colors are made up of the same components as other similar colors. Most of the colors are made of different metals and materials, mixed with a solution that allows the colors to spread in an even and consistent way allowing the ink to look full, bright, and spread in to the skin, the exact way the needle wants it to spread. It's extremely important to pick the right ink; I spare no expense with my inks. The best inks on the markets are the common Intense, Starbright, And MOMS. Also I have to give mention to my new favorite is it's called Dermoglow. It's from the UK and it's simply the best ink I have ever used, the blue is amazing

Below is a small list of what certain colors are made of:

BLACK: Made of iron oxides, carbon, or logwood.

BROWNS, FLESHTONES: Made of ochre.

RED: Made of cinnabar, cadmium red, iron oxide, or napthol.

ORANGE: Made of disazodiarylide, disazopyrazolone, or cadmium seleno-sulfide.

YELLOW Made of cadmium yellow, ochres, curcuma yellow, chrome yellow, or disazodiarylide.

GREEN: Made of chromium oxide ("Casalis Green" or "Anadomis Green"), Malachite, Ferrocyanides, Ferricyanides, Lead chromate, Monoazo pigment, Cu/Al phthalocyanine, or Cu phthalocyanine.

BLUE: Made of azure blue, cobalt blue, or Cu-phtalocyanine.

VIOLET: Made of manganese violet (manganese ammonium pyrophosphate), quinacridone, dioxazine/carbazole, and various aluminum salts.

WHITE - Made of lead white (lead carbonate), titanium dioxide, barium sulfate, or zinc oxide.

It's always a good idea to use disposable ink caps. This prevents contamination of the ink from one client to the next. The ink is not reused, and any excess is thrown away.

Chapter 6: Designing/Sketching

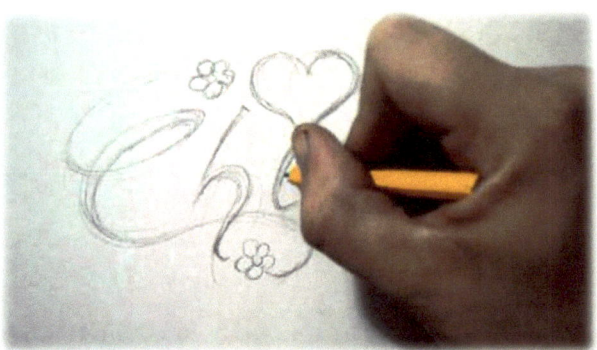

A very important part of tattooing is making sure that the customer is happy with the outcome & the final work of their tattoo when it is all healed. It's important to make sure that the design makes sense for the customer, there are many things to take in to consideration: The location of their body they want the tattoo, what kind of coloring/shading they are looking for and the size. Another thing to keep in mind is the color variation depending on the particular person's skin. Different colors show differently on different skin colors & textures. You will learn which skins take which inks and colors best through experience, as you tattoo all of your friends, family, locals and hopefully eventually, people from all over the world.

Most people come in with ideas in their heads, or pieces of what it is they want tattooed on them. It's a good idea to make a few different sketches of the ideas and let the customer pick & choose what they like and what they don't like to help both of you in the direction you are taking the tattoo. After you have gone over the sizing, the positioning & the shading of the tattoo the final sketch is ready to go you are ready to move on to transferring it over to the tattoo paper.

Chapter 7: Tracing design to the transfer Paper

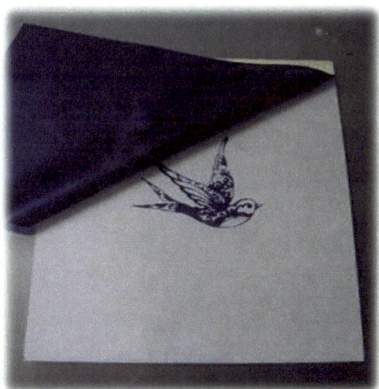

Now you have your sketch & outline drawn out, your customer is getting more excited and anxious to get started. There are still a few mores steps to do before your customer starts getting zapped. To transfer your final sketch on to the Transfer paper is a very simple yet a very tedious task that is important because it will be the basic outline of the initial tattooing, although you can still fix a few things freehand as you go along, it is still important to have a good sketch traced on the transfer paper. You want to trace the sketch on to the transfer paper, usually found at Tattoo supply shops/websites. There are two ways of doing this, you can use a thermal copier machine, or you can trace by hand. This depends on how you prefer to do it, the tattoo & if you have access to a copier at the time. If you do have a Thermal Copier, you simply place your sketch between the carbon paper & the transfer paper and run it through the machine; it will make a perfect copy of the sketch on the transfer paper allowing you to be able to place it on the skin. If you do not have access to a Thermal copier you can trace it yourself. The first thing you will need to do is remove the little brown protective paper in the middle of the carbon & sketch paper. Set the original sketch on top of the white sheet of transfer paper and firmly trace the outline. It's recommended to use a bold point or a ball point pen when tracing, using a fine point will probably be too sharp and cause the paper to rip.

Chapter 8: Preparing & sterilizing the skin

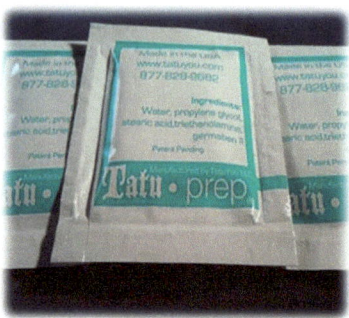 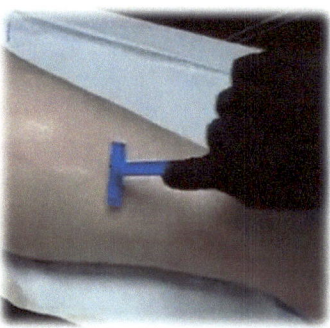

Now that you have finished your final design and got it on your transfer paper, it's time to transfer it on to the skin where you will be doing the tattoo. You want to make sure that skin is clean & free of any hair. This is so the client doesn't end up with ingrown hairs during the healing process. Even if the skin appears to be bald already, it's always a good precaution to have a Brand new razor, some warm water & some good shaving cream to be sure that it doesn't get irritated. A small nick in the skin can be a burden to the tattoo & you don't want irritated skin where you're going to be tattooing, so be sure you add plenty of warm water and shaving cream. Once it's all shaved & smooth, you will then clean it with either a alcohol pad or some green soap & water. After cleaning, Apply the stencil, using a Ultrasonic gel, some people use unscented Speed stick deodorant. Ultrasonic gel is the same gel that they use in ultra sounds in the medical field, it will help transfer the design from the paper to the skin, the deodorant stick does the same thing, just be sure it is the green unscented speed stick deodorant. When applying the paper to the skin you want to be sure the applied area is relaxed, and resting. Tense muscles can cause the design to look out of alignment when the muscles relax in normal position, making the tattoo look a little misplaced.

Transferring design to the skin

A lot of people prefer to use Speed stick deodorant to transfer the design on to the skin. You can use this or you can Ultrasonic gel usually used for ultra sounds in the medical field. What it is you prefer, the procedure is pretty much the same concept. You apply the paper to the skin allowing and pressing firmly with the ink side is facing downward so the design can be printed on the skin. Apply a nice amount of pressure to the skin, allowing the design to transfer. You peel back slowly, while apply pressure to the areas need. This should allow the outline to be printed pretty clearly on the skin and give you a good starting point to start doing the tattoo.

Chapter 9: Preparing the Tattoo Machine & Workstation

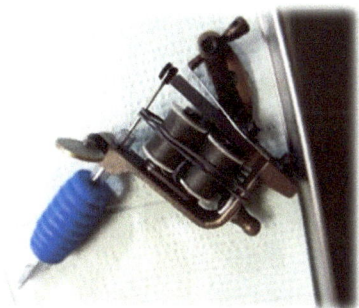

Anything that you will touch throughout the process of the tattoo, you want to make sure is covered in plastic to prevent cross contamination from any body fluids. Anything that you will be making contact with is covered in plastic or disposable. All needles are autoclave sterilized, though they should never be used twice. This includes anything is in contact of your general area. You want to make sure lights are covered, seats, chairs, benches, work station area, your tools, anything that could potentially be hazardous of airborne or physical germs and/or diseases.

You will need:

1. New clean latex gloves.
2. New sterilized needles
3. New sterilized tubes.
4. New ink and inkcaps.
5. Uses new salve and spatula

Chapter 10: Tattoo Procedure

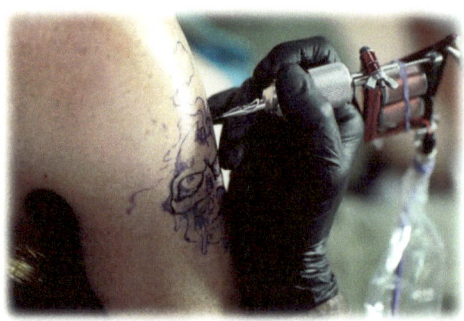

Before beginning double check that you are comfortable in your chair and your client is as well, you guys will be here for a while, so if you need some refreshments, grab them now!

Outlining:

Remember the outline is the foundation for building the rest of the tattoo. If the outline isn't good the rest of the tattoo won't be either. Always make sure to check over your machine first and make sure everything is in order before getting started.

When working with a client the artist should try to gauge the person's reaction to the initial needle poke. Some people are squeamish and others just don't feel it. If this is the person's first tattoo, care should be taken to pick an area of the outline where little damage can be one if the client pulls away or moves suddenly during the initial lining. It's very important to help the customer be comfortable; assuring them that everything is ok, or asking them if they are ok. Some customer don't feel anything at all, some are very scared/sensitive, most of the time it is just their nerves so just communicate with them and all should be ok. Lining can make or break a tattoo. The line must be straight and clean. A light hand of the improper needle depth can be the difference between a very blotchy, dotted looking blurry ugly line, from a clean straight line. It's also very important to be sure to stretch the skin that you are tattooing, allowing a tight solid surface for the need to penetrate and to make sure skin doesn't get blotchy.

Before getting started with the outline it's a good idea to keep a few guidelines in mind first.

Always tattoo forward or sideways with the machine. This ensures the needles always have a backward pressure so there will be a continual flow of ink in the machine tube.

Keeping the skin pulled tight is very important in getting a clean tattoo, tattooing on loose skin will leave bad end results.

The first step in beginning your outline is to dip the machine tip into the outlining color, which is normally black. This should be done before the machine is ever even turned on. The reservoir should be filled with ink so you can continue for a little while and create the first few lines easily.

Begin your outlining from the bottom of the design and work your way up. After the first few initial lines are done, be sure to stop and see what they look like to ensure there are no problems such as faint lines, etc. After this you'll need to dip the tip into the ink several times to get the outline accomplished. Work to make your lines in one long motion. Remember to fill the tip every few seconds to avoid running dry. Avoid pressing too hard and always start at the top of a line.

After the tattoo outline is complete you can step back and take a break. Be sure to check it to ensure there is no need for touchups. Now you're ready to continue with the rest of the tattoo, which is shading.

Shading

Generally shading with black is known as shadowing. This type of work is very eye-catching and attractive. Unfortunately, if the black shading is not done correctly it can really be the downfall of the tattoo. There is definitely an art form to learning to shade correctly. Black is a very bold color and it is important to master the appropriate techniques of shading. Besides simply applying black on the skin, to learn to shade right you need to learn the idea behind light and shadow to create a realistic shadow. This requires practice and lots time put in to it. It there is one area that you need to master this would be it.

Always remember you can correct a wide variety of mistakes if you are able to shadow and shade with black. In fact, in the tattoo industry, artists are often judged by how well they can shade and shadow with black.

Basic Steps to Shading

Remember to use a 7 Mags or 11 Mags needle shader as well as the proper tube, with the needles sticking out 1/32 of an inch from the tip. Usually I keep the needles flat with the opening of the tube, it helps to keep sure the needle doesn't snag the skin.

To start a shadow, begin with the lightest areas first and then work your way toward the darkest areas, Developing the contrast. My method is to use 4 cups. The first cup has 1 drop of ink the next cup 10 drops the third cup is half full with ink and the 4th cups is full of black ink, then I fill the cups the rest of the way with witch hazel.

Remember to work in circular motions but make sure you don't overwork it or you'll have black ink everywhere.

A technique known as sweep shading is used for both color and black shading. The tip of the tattoo machine is moved forward. As you move forward you will need to flick your wrist upward. Remember the sweep shading method requires extensive practice to get it right. It is important to make sure you get this technique right because it is often used for larger tattoos that require a lot of color and intricate designs.

To set up for sweep shading you will need to set the needles further apart. Instead of setting them at 1/32" they will need to be set at 1/16". Increasing the depth will provide the depth needed for color.

To achieve a good color shading make sure you maintain constant, flowing and tight circles. Avoid shading an area more than once to avoid doing damage to the skin. Try not to press too hard on the needle tube as you move it over the area. When you complete an area, be sure to wipe it and then check to see if any touchups are required. Make sure you wipe away the excess ink so you can check the area that should be shaded.

There is a guideline when it comes to the order in which you be applying color. If you don't follow the order correctly, this can cause a lot of color clashing and covering up colors and cause that tattoo to have bad coloring.

The proper order is as follows:

Dark purple

Blues

Greens

Light Purple

Browns

Reds

Orange

Yellow

White

There are a few tips to coloring, one tip is making sure you allow some time between color shading, this allows the previous color to dry, so when you apply a new color the tattoo will not become blurred or smeared, leaving accurate and clean coloring.

The next tip is to make sure that you use a lot of ointment as you go along adding color; this will help keep the colors from mixing on the skin, kind of like a barrier from color to color.

Chapter 11: After session

After tattoo is complete, you need to dispose of all waste in a Biohazard containment unit, this includes: used needles, paper towels, and any plastic covering your work station.

Clean the customers arm using green soap and water wiping firmly to be sure any loose ink and/or blood wipes off.

Cover the open wound in A & D ointment and wrap the tattoo in plastic, instructing client to leave it on for about 2 hours.

After two hours has passed, you will remove the plastic and clean it with soap and water, not applying too much pressure.

You also want to make you let your customer know that you don't want them to scrub the tattoo with a towel or any type of wash cloth, but you want them to simply use soap and water and rub the tattoo, firmly, but carefully with their hand. It helps keep the ink in order so there is no smearing.

After the tattoo session has been completed you will need to sterilize and your work station your tools away. This is very important because it ensure safety and organization. Be sure to place your machines in an Ultrasonic Cleaner for at least 30 minutes and wipe down everything handled during the procedure. The floor of the area should also be mopped and all trash taken out. Remember to close the bags and staple them.

After you remove the needle bars and glass tubes from the Cleaner they will need to scrub. After drying it off and then checking it to ensure there is no excessive wear it can be reused.

Sterilization should be your NUMBER ONE priority! If you don't, you can not only get in a lot of trouble and be put out of business, but you also run into many huge health issues

Chapter 12: Finding an apprenticeship:

Finding an apprentice ship can be hard. Shops are either full or are afraid to take the risk of having a new apprentice around. You have to understand that shops are often too busy to have a trainee around; it takes time, and risk that someone could leave with a bad tattoo. If you looking for an apprenticeship, you have to realize you're in a position on making the tattoo shop owner feel like it's worth their time and that you are trustworthy. You will defiantly need to have some art skills. The last thing any shop owner wants is to put some hacker on the street with a tattoo machine. Bad artists or should I say bad work ethic has caused some shops to not even want to deal with apprentices. So surely make sure you let them feel that you're trustworthy and willing to work hard and learn. **AND DO SOME HARD WORK!**

Chapter 13: Setting up your Own Tattoo Shop

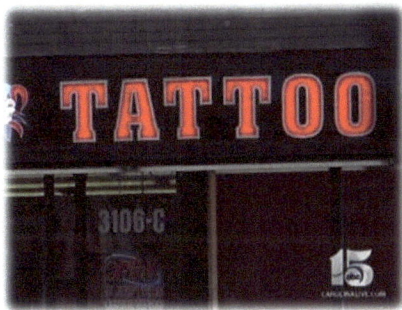

When you are first starting off doing tattoos, you probably will be doing them in the privacy of your own home, regardless of where you are doing them, you always to keep focused on sanitation. This will allow you to be able gain the practice, using the right guidelines & procedures, getting used to doing things the right way, so when you do move on to a shop you aren't learning to do things correctly, you've been doing it correctly the whole time. Plus, you don't want your family and friends being exposed to dangers of unsafe tattooing.

When it does come time to set up your own shop, there are a few things to keep in mind when picking your location.

You are going to need space for a waiting room, restroom, private tattoo room and a work room to keep your equipment and tools.

If you are serious about starting your OWN tattoo business, you will need a good tattoo business plan

When setting up prices, you want to make sure you cover the cost of your supplies, equipment, and if you have your own shop then you will have other expenses as well. Keeping all of this in mind, you want to make sure you charging your clients enough to help you cover all of those costs, plus making a living. Keeping that in mind, you want your prices to be reasonable and consistent. Get an idea of what the local competition is charging and also the quality of their work. A lot of shops base their prices off of categories, such as sizes, color, lettering, etc. Many shops find it handy to create price specific categories, usually according to the size of the tattoo. Depending on the location of where they want the tattoo, it's always good to make a few different sizes, and let them know what you want for the smallest size, and from there they are more likely going to pick the biggest tattoo, which means more income for your shop!

Following local laws & ordinances

Always be sure you are following all local laws and safety codes. This is very important as it could ruin your business completely. Double check all laws and codes to be sure, to prevent any disasters and if you should have a surprise visitor they will be pleased with your shop and maybe even want some work done!

This includes zoning, permits and licenses.

Managing the books

Finally, be sure to keep your books up to date and handle the tracking of your income and expenses precisely for tax purposes. Using technology to you benefit is a good thing, using things like spreadsheets, quickbooks accounting software & even calendars allowing everything to be kept up to date, while maintaining record of everything. If you are using a computer to do everything on, it is always safe to have a backup Hard drive and/or computer to help archive old data safely, I always find it safe to have everything twice, so if something tragic happens to one computer or hard drive, you may lose recent information but all old records are stored in a second, safe location.

The more organized you are with things like this, the easier tax time is ☺

Promoting your shop online

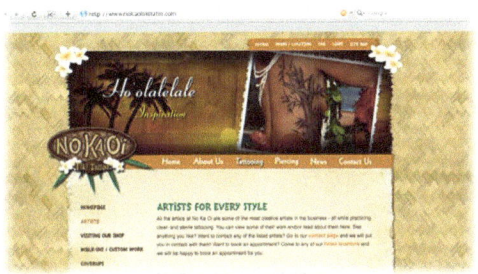

If you plan to make a lot of money you have to be up with the time and the hot thing now is the internet. You will need a website. Google places account. And if you really want to engage your clients you will need a Facebook page and twitter. All of your clients are there so why shouldn't you be? There are tons of ways to get traffic to your website. Asking your customers and to get involved and ask them to like you on Facebook, we offer a $5 coupon every time people like our page. Now we have thousands of likes and our clients and local residents sharing our links and coupons. This keeps us super busy once it's all setup and working. We do the same for Google places and reviews. Give them and deal or a coupon and you will have no problem getting social media attention. This works great the more you use it. **That's the road to a 6 figure income!** Get your customers involved, let them know that you care and you're there and they will be happy.

Also, I can't stress enough a Great way to get local client's fast. Make a nice "professional" ad and post on craigslist it can bring you instant customers. I've done this for years. Make sure your ad is clean and professional. I landed a client that bought a sleeve tattoo worth $1500.00 my first week being open like this! Whenever its gets a little slow post, post, post!

Portfolio

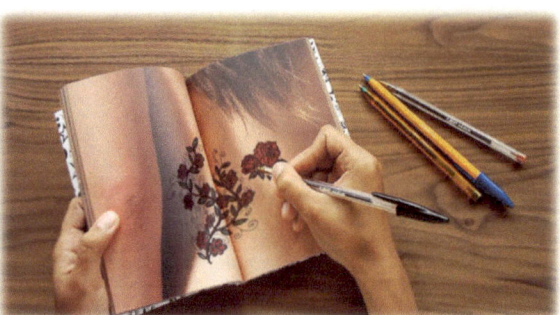

Make sure you have a nice clean up to date portfolio. Your portfolio and how it's displayed is everything, its and extension of your art and people pay extreme attention to it.Put yourself in the clients shoes if you walk into a shop and the place smells or isn't clean or upkept, you think they're going to want someone there to penetrate their skin? Doubt it.

Your portfolio can make the different from commanding $50 a tattoo or $100 for the same tattoo. I'd rather have my work displayed nice and look clean and trim & command the higher price.

That's the road to a 6 figure income!

Customer service

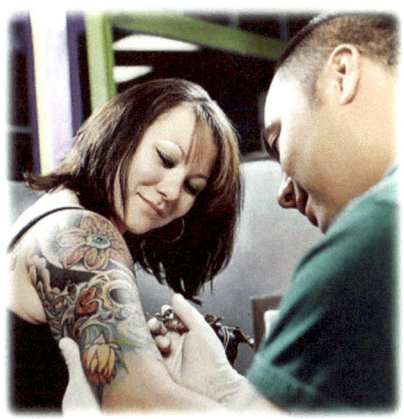

I can't stress this enough, you want to make six figure tattooing?
Well, listen up customer service is everything.

If you're not a people person well you may be in trouble, it's hard for people to support you if you like to hide under a rock. Or you could have everyone in town at your door because you're the nicest guy to get a tattoo from. People are nervous about artists in general sometimes. With the bad wrap tattoo artists used to get. But now it's changed. But you do still have to deal with People who are nervous before getting there tattoo. It's the cool calm collected artist that puts them at ease. Tattooing is a BIG BIG deal for a lot of people. You treat your client right and they're yours for life. In tattooing you can develop a near cult like following. People love to stick with the same tattooist and for good reason. Provide good customer service and you have accomplished a monumental setup.

That's the road to a 6 figure income!

Picking a shop name

Another often overlooked part of the road to six figures tattooing. Let me ask you one thing, If you and Mom and your looking to live a little and get a tattoo. You have $200 bucks in your pocket and you arrive on the Venice beach strip and you see tattoo shop names #1 "Dead Man Walking Tattoos". Shop #2 "Evil

Needles Tattoo" Or the shop #3 'The Tattoo Gallery'. Which choice do you think this person will make? The name of your shop is extremely important in business. There are many shops that you would think a 16 year old teen was smoking pot and picked out the name. A bad name can mean the end to a otherwise successful business.

In closing

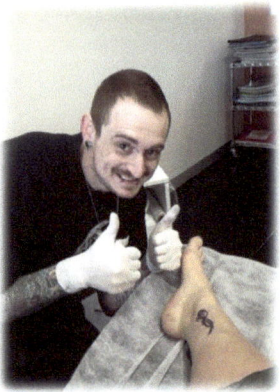

    We have gone over many things that will help you be a successful artist and be on the road to a six figure income. Our next installment is around the corner. We will go into Online marketing even more and how to setup your website and social media pages. One thing I want to add before we end: All of this useful information is useless if you don't have the drive to make six figures? You will have to be able to get back up and do what you have to do. Sleeping in to 12:00 pm every day won't make you successful even if you think that's a tattoo artist's life. That's a tattoo artist's life that makes 10k a year. If you want to make the big money you will have to apply these things and if something does not work, try to change things and try again. There are a few tattoo artists that will make 1-2 million dollars a year in 2012. It's because **they work hard** applied the methods and then continuing making more revenue selling, shirts or selling artwork both Online and offline.

There's tons of money out there. Go get some!

THE ULTIMATE TATTOO TRAINING GUIDE

How to Create a Six Figure Income!